SUPER
BIKES

Author:

Ian Graham was born
in Belfast in 1953. He studied
applied physics at The City
University, London, and took
a postgraduate diploma in
journalism at the same
university, specialising in
science and technology
journalism. After four years
as an editor of consumer
electronics magazines, he
became a freelance author and
journalist. Since then, he has
written more than one hundred
children's non-fiction books and
numerous magazine articles.

Artist:

Nick Hewetson was
born in Surrey in 1958. He was
educated in Sussex at Brighton
Technical School and studied
illustration at Eastbourne
College of Art. He has since
illustrated a wide variety of
children's books.

Editor:

Stephen Haynes

Editorial Assistant:

Mark Williams

PAPER FROM
SUSTAINABLE
FORESTS

SALARIYA

Published in Great Britain MMIX by
Book House, an imprint of
The Salariya Book Company Ltd
25 Marlborough Place, Brighton, BNI IUB
www.salariya.com
www.book-house.co.uk

PB ISBN 978-1-906714-52-9

A CIP Catalogue record for this book is available
from the British Library.

Printed and bound in China.
Printed on paper from sustainable sources.

Visit our website at **www.book-house.co.uk** or
www.salariya.com for **free** electronic versions of:
You Wouldn't Want to be an Egyptian Mummy!
You Wouldn't Want to be a Roman Gladiator!
Avoid Joining Shackleton's Polar Expedition!
Avoid Sailing on a 19th-Century Whaling Ship!

This book is adapted from *Super Bikes* by
Ian Graham, created, designed and
produced by The Salariya Book Company
and published by Hodder Wayland in
MMI in the Fast Forward series.

SUPER BIKES

Written by
IAN GRAHAM

Illustrated by
NICK HEWETSON

Created and designed by
DAVID SALARIYA

BOOK HOUSE

Contents

▶ France, 1869: Michaux brothers' steam-driven bicycle.

Early Motorcycles

Steam-powered bicycles were built in the 19th century. Their **fuel** (coal or wood) was heavy and bulky. It took a long time to make enough steam to move the vehicle. Petrol engines, developed in the 1880s, were much better.

▼ USA, 1880s: Copeland brothers' steam bicycle.

▼ Germany, 1885: Gottlieb Daimler (below) and Wilhelm Maybach fitted a small petrol engine to a wooden bicycle with stabilisers. It could reach a top speed of 19 kph (12 mph).

Daimler–Maybach motorcycle, 1885

Germany, 1901:
NSU motorcycle

▼ The NSU's 234 **cc**,
1.5 **horsepower**
engine had a
top speed of
50 kph
(30 mph).

▼ USA, 1904: The Indian
Single, made by the racing
cyclists George Hendee and
Oscar Hedstrom. 'Indian'
motorcycles were known for their
good design and workmanship.

Cylinder

Battery

Exhaust
pipe

Indian Single

INDIAN

Japan, 1940s:
Suzuki
Power Free

▼ Suzuki's first motorbike
had a tiny 36 cc engine.
It was clipped on to an
ordinary bicycle frame.

Drive belt

Stabiliser wheels

7

Grand Prix

Motorcycle racing became popular in the early 1900s. *Grand Prix* is French for 'big prize'. The biggest prize in bike racing is the MotoGP World Championship.

1956 MV Agusta Four: top speed 250 kph (155 mph)

◀ John Surtees was seven times World Champion in the late 1950s. He then became the Formula 1 car-racing champion in 1964.

A 1960s Grand Prix race

Tyres are heated before a race. The soft rubber grips best when it is warm.

Electric blanket

◀ Barry Sheene, 500 cc World Champion in 1976 and 1977.

Kenny Roberts, the first American World Champion (1978, 1979, 1980).

British-made bikes were the most successful until the 1950s. Then Italian bikes dominated the sport until the 1970s. Japanese bikes then took the lead.

9

11

Stunt Riders

Don't try this at home! These extreme sports are very dangerous. Stunts are carefully planned by teams of professionals, but accidents still happen. Evel Knievel is said to have broken nearly every bone in his body.

▲ ▶ Evel Knievel's son Robbie made a spectacular jump over the Grand Canyon in 1999. He jumped a record-breaking distance of 70 m (230 ft) through the air. He crashed after landing, breaking two of his ribs and spraining his ankle.

Take-off ramp

▲ Evel Knievel was the world's best-known motorcycle stunt rider. His most famous jumps include a leap over 50 cars. In 1974 he tried to jump across the Snake River Canyon in Idaho using a rocket-powered Harley-Davidson 'skycycle'. A parachute accidentally popped out on take-off, and he floated safely to the ground.

▲ Motorcycle skiing is one of the most dangerous stunts. Showers of sparks fly from the rider's steel-soled boots.

▶ Angelle Seeling is one of the few female drag riders.

▲ A winner celebrating with a high-speed wheelie.

13

15

The Yamaha YZF-R1 is light and powerful. The whole machine weighs only 177 kg (390 lb). Almost every part is made of thinner material than usual. The handlebars are glued on to save the weight of the bolts! The four-**cylinder** engine is more powerful than many car engines, at 150 **bhp** (**brake horsepower**). It has a top speed of 280 kph (174 mph). ▶

Ducati 996

Rear view of the YZF-R1

Lightweight **titanium silencer**

Front view of the YZF-R1

Fuel tank

Engine

DELTABOX II

YAMAHA

Streamlined engine **fairing**

Slimmed-down **disc brakes**

Yamaha YZF-R1

◀ The Italian Ducati 996 is a streamlined road bike. It has a 996 cc engine and lightweight **tubular frame**. Its top speed is 260 kph (162 mph). British racer Carl Fogarty won four World Superbike Championships on Ducatis in the 1990s.

Handlebars

YZF

YAMAHA

Lightweight
3-spoke wheels

Mean Machines

These high-performance road bikes are built to look like racing machines. Engine power, a highly streamlined shape and light weight are the key factors.

Suzuki TL1000R

▲ The Suzuki TL1000R's 1000 cc **V-twin** engine has a top speed of more than 240 kph (150 mph).

▼ A 900 cc four-cylinder engine takes the Fireblade's speed up to 265 kph (165 mph).

Honda Fireblade

▼ Cal Rayborn won the Daytona 200 in 1968 and 1969. In 1970 he set a motorcycle land speed record of 427 kph (265 mph).

Superstars

Motorcycle sports really put riders and their bikes to the test. Long-distance endurance races last up to 24 hours. Teams of two or three riders take turns on one bike. Superbike racing, using modified road bikes, is hugely popular.

▼ A **pit stop**. A fast turnaround can make all the difference between winning and losing.

◀ Carl Fogarty is a superbike champion. Superbikes are very similar to road bikes.

A good pit team can refuel and change tyres and riders in just a few seconds.

A superbike in action

20

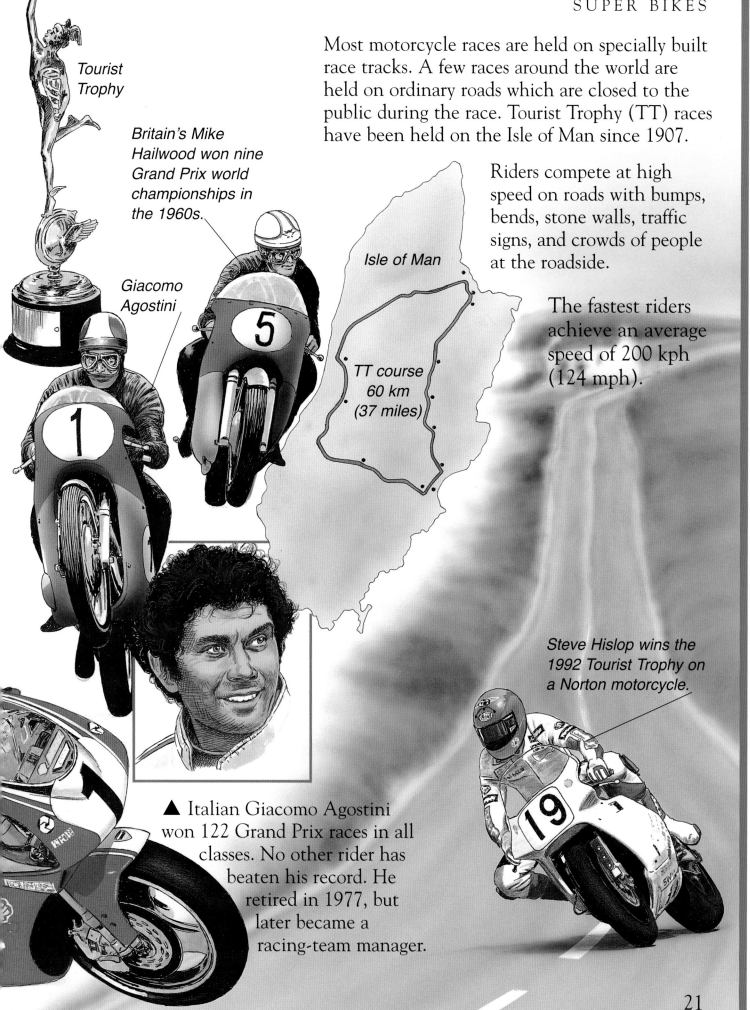

Tourist Trophy

Britain's Mike Hailwood won nine Grand Prix world championships in the 1960s.

Giacomo Agostini

Most motorcycle races are held on specially built race tracks. A few races around the world are held on ordinary roads which are closed to the public during the race. Tourist Trophy (TT) races have been held on the Isle of Man since 1907.

Isle of Man

TT course 60 km (37 miles)

Riders compete at high speed on roads with bumps, bends, stone walls, traffic signs, and crowds of people at the roadside.

The fastest riders achieve an average speed of 200 kph (124 mph).

Steve Hislop wins the 1992 Tourist Trophy on a Norton motorcycle.

▲ Italian Giacomo Agostini won 122 Grand Prix races in all classes. No other rider has beaten his record. He retired in 1977, but later became a racing-team manager.

Dirt Devils

Motorcycles are raced on every type of surface. Loose surfaces like sand, dirt and **shale** are difficult because the tyres have nothing to grip. Riders often have to put a foot down for support.

Motocross rider

Motocross bike

Husqvarna

610

▼ Speedway bikes are light and low. They have no brakes. They are designed for fast acceleration. Desert bikes are bigger, and up to four times as heavy. They are higher off the ground and have bigger fuel tanks.

Desert bike

Speedway bike

◀ American Jeremy McGrath won the national Supercross Championship seven times between 1993 and 2000. He has been racing bikes since the age of 5.

Desert racing

Trial bikes have no seats. They are ridden over obstacles such as rocks and tree trunks.

▼ Motocross bikes have very springy suspension to help keep them level on bumpy, muddy courses.

▲ The most famous desert race is the Dakar Rally, across the Sahara Desert in North Africa. Getting lost in the desert is dangerous. Groups of riders often stay within sight of each other for safety.

HUSQVARNA

1

4 T C

Husqvarna

▶ *Ice-racing bikes have tyres covered in steel spikes for grip. It would be impossible to lean into a corner without them.*

Spiked tyre

▶ *The fastest way to corner in speedway racing is to lean the bike over and let the back wheel swing out sideways.*

Steel-soled boot

23

Honda
X-Wing

Suzuki
TL1000S

▲ The 1500 cc
X-Wing is a **prototype**
'super-scooter'. It
combines engineering
with rider comfort.

▶ Designers
like to produce
bold ideas of
what future
bikes might
look like.

What Next?

Motorcycle design is always developing. New materials such as **carbon fibre** make bikes lighter, so they need less power and use less fuel. Engines are becoming more efficient too, and streamlining reduces air resistance.

▼ A futuristic design based on a real motorcycle, the 1000 cc Suzuki TL1000S sports road bike.

▼ Some manufacturers like to use technical and engineering developments from the racetrack to improve their road bikes. French designer Philippe Starck wanted to combine advanced technology with a look that would not go out of date. The result was the Aprilia Moto 6.5.

Aprilia Moto 6.5

Driver's cab

▲ This giant **replica** of a Harley-Davidson is 14 m (46 ft) long and weighs 5 tonnes. A Cadillac car engine gives it a top speed of 130 kph (80 mph).

◄ Some people prefer new bikes that look like old ones. This classic Harley-Davidson design is especially popular.

25

A full-face helmet protects the head, face and jaw. Air vents keep the head cool and stop the visor misting up.

Visor

► Leather outer suit. Extra protection can be worn under it to shield areas such as the hips.

'Slider' (knee pad)

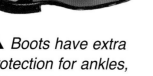

▲ Boots have extra protection for ankles, shins and toes.

26

Bike Safety

It is vital that motorcyclists protect themselves from injury by wearing the right clothing. A helmet has a soft lining that cushions the head. This stops the skull being fractured or crushed if there is an accident. Leathers protect against cuts and scrapes.

All-in-one suits are called 'leathers'. They provide some protection if the rider comes off the bike and slides along the track. Leather is good because when it is scraped along the ground it wears away, but does not tear.

A slider pad protects the rider's knee as it touches the ground on corners.

Reinforced gloves

Leathers

▲ A loss of tyre grip can easily spill the rider onto the track.

Full-face helmet

Full-face helmet

Tear-resistant jacket

Leather gloves

Armoured jeans

Armoured jeans have tough pads sewn into the material. They protect the rider in case of an accident.

Boots support the toes and ankles. Some protect the shins, too.

Useful Words

Brake horsepower (bhp)
A measurement of engine power.

Carbon fibre
A solid, strong and light material used to make safety helmets and parts of motorcycles.

cc
Cubic centimetres – a measurement of the size of an engine's cylinders.

Cylinder
One of the tube-shaped chambers in an engine where fuel is burned.

Disc brakes
Brakes that work by using pads to grip a steel disc fixed to the wheel.

Drag racers
Motorcyclists who race powerful machines down a short, straight course, two at a time.

Fairing
A streamlined covering that wraps around the front of a motorcycle.

Fuel
A liquid such as petrol that is burned inside an engine.

Horsepower
A measurement of engine power.

Kevlar
A tough man-made material used in clothing for motorcyclists.

Pit stop
A visit to the pits (garages at the side of a racetrack), where bikes can be refuelled and tyres or riders changed.

Production bike
A bike which is made in large numbers and can be ridden on an ordinary road.

Prototype
The first version of a new bike design. It is used to test the design before more bikes are made.

Replica
An exact copy.

Shale
A fine, gravelly rock.

Silencer
A pipe-shaped chamber attached to an engine's exhaust pipe to reduce engine noise.

Single
A bike with a one-cylinder engine.

Streamlined
Made with a smooth shape that slips easily through the air.

Titanium
An extremely tough, light metal that does not rust and can stand very high temperatures.

Tubular frame
A motorcycle frame made from metal tubes welded together.

V-twin
An engine with two cylinders joined in a V-shape.

Milestones

1869 The French Michaux brothers add a small steam engine to a bicycle and build the first motorised two-wheeled vehicle.

1885 Gottlieb Daimler and Wilhelm Maybach build the first petrol-engined motorcycle.

1894 The first mass-produced motorcycle is manufactured by Heinrich Hildebrand and Alois Wolfmüller.

1902 The first motor scooter is built in France.

1904 The first Harley-Davidson motorcycle, called the 'Silent Gray Fellow', is made in the USA.

1909 The first motorcycle speed record, 122 kph (76 mph), is set by William Cook at Brooklands racetrack in England.

1912 New Yorker Carl Stevens Clancy becomes the first person to ride a motorcycle around the world.

1920 The first official motorcycle land speed record, 167 kph (104 mph), is set by Ernie Walker.

1974 Evel Knievel's attempt to jump his rocket-powered motorcycle over the Snake River Canyon in Idaho fails.

1975 Italian Giacomo Agostini wins the 500 cc Grand Prix championship for the eighth and final time.

1978 Donald Vesco sets a motorcycle land speed record of 512 kph (318 mph) on his *Lightning Bolt*, a specially built machine powered by two Kawasaki motorcycle engines.

1983 The first rocket-propelled motorcycle is built by Dutch drag racer Henk Vink. It can reach a top speed of 400 kph (248 mph).

2000 Robbie Knievel jumps his motorcycle over a moving railway locomotive.

2002 The old 500 cc Grand Prix class is replaced by MotoGP, allowing engines up to 990 cc.

2005 Italian Valentino Rossi wins his seventh Grand Prix World Championship.

2006 The motorcycle land speed record is broken twice in three days, first by Rocky Robinson (551.678 kph/342.797 mph), then by Chris Carr (564.693 kph/ 350.884 mph).

2007 MotoGP bikes are limited to an engine capacity of 800 cc.

Index